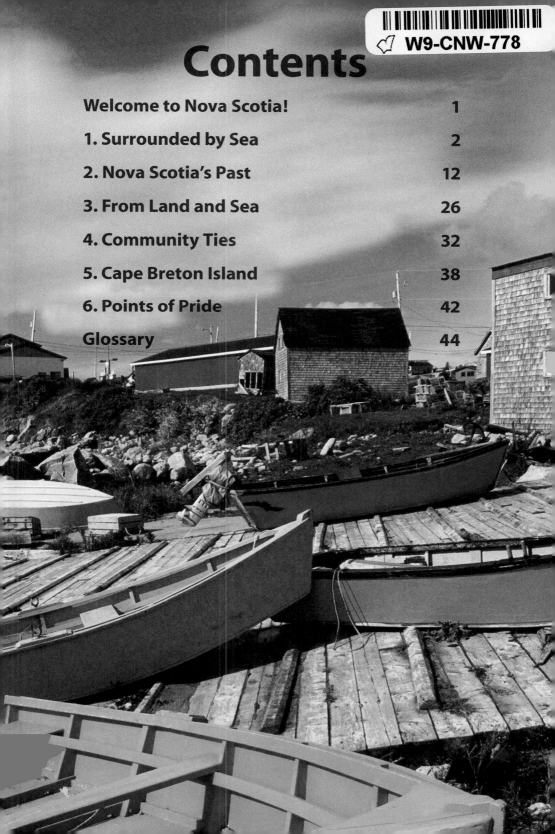

Contents

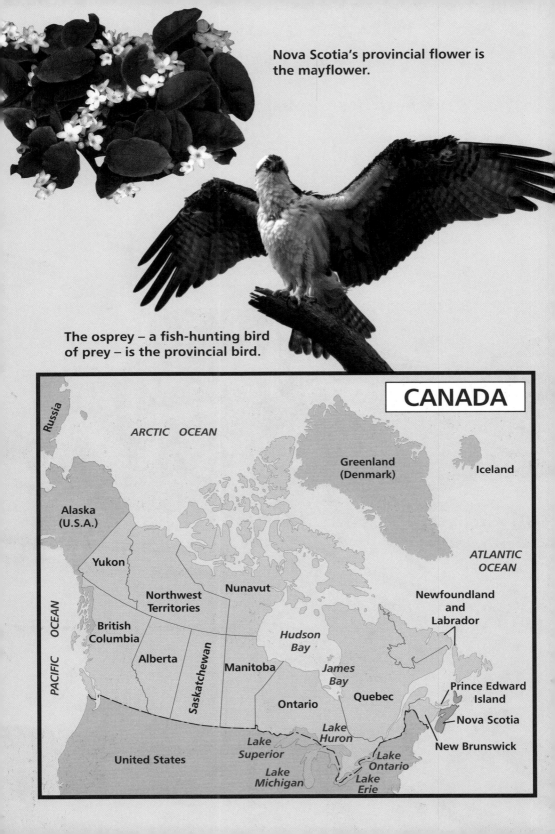

Nova Scotia's provincial flower is the mayflower.

The osprey – a fish-hunting bird of prey – is the provincial bird.

CANADA

Russia

ARCTIC OCEAN

Greenland (Denmark)

Iceland

Alaska (U.S.A.)

Yukon

ATLANTIC OCEAN

PACIFIC OCEAN

Northwest Territories

Nunavut

Newfoundland and Labrador

British Columbia

Hudson Bay

Alberta

Saskatchewan

Manitoba

James Bay

Quebec

Prince Edward Island

Ontario

Nova Scotia

New Brunswick

Lake Huron

Lake Superior

Lake Ontario

United States

Lake Michigan

Lake Erie

Nova Scotia

Carrie Gleason

Scholastic Canada Ltd.
**Toronto New York London Auckland Sydney
Mexico City New Delhi Hong Kong Buenos Aires**

Canada Close Up

Visual Credits

Cover: Rolf Hicker/AllCanadaPhotos.com; p. I: Lowell Georgia/Corbis; p. III: Radius Images/ AllCanadaPhotos.com; p. IV: (top left) Deni Bown Dorling Kindersley, (middle) Craig Hanson/ Shutterstock Inc.; p.2: Heeb Christian/Maxx Images; p. 3: John Sylvester/AllCanadaPhotos.com; p. 4: (top) Yva Momatiuk & John Eastcott/Minden Pictures/National Geographic Stock; p. 5: (top and middle) Kasia/Shutterstock Inc., (bottom) Creatas/SuperStock; p. 6: Darwin Wiggett/AllCanadaPhotos. com; p. 7: (top) Ultrashock/Shutterstock Inc., (bottom) Greg Toope/Shutterstock Inc.; p. 8: (middle) Phil Degginger/Alamy, (bottom left) Stefanie Mohr Photography/Shutterstock Inc., (bottom right) eAlisa/ Shutterstock Inc.; p. 9: (top) William Albert Allard/National Geographic Stock, (bottom) Brock May/ Photoresearchers/First Light; p. 10: Blaine Harrington III/Alamy; p. 11 and back cover: S Duffett/ Shutterstock Inc.; p. 13: (top) McCord Museum M11443, (bottom) Portrait Essentials/Alamy; p. 14: McCord Museum MP-0000.4.14; p. 15: North Wind/North Wind Picture Archives; p. 16: (top) The Print Collector/Alamy, (bottom) Alan Keohane Dorling Kindersley; p. 18: North Wind/North Wind Picture Archives; p. 19: Hemis/Alamy; p. 20: (top) Russ Heinl/AllCanadaPhotos.com, (bottom) Stephen Saks Photography/Alamy; p. 21: J. Stanger, Duncan McLennan, Arch. McLennan, A. MacPherson, Licenced Passenger Brokers/Glenbow Archives; p. 22: (top) Library and Archives Canada; Copyright: Canada Post Corporation {1984}. Reproduced with Permission, (bottom) Chris Lund/National Film Board/Library and Archives Canada/PA-152023; p. 23: (both) Bettmann/CORBIS; p. 24: Canada. Patent and Copyright Office/Library and Archives Canada/PA-030304; p. 25: Henry Georgi/AllCanadaPhotos. com; p. 26: (top) Rolf Hicker Photography/AllCanadaPhotos.com, (bottom) Willy Matheisl/Maxx Images; p. 27: (top left) Morgan Lane Photography/Shutterstock Inc., (top right) Richard Griffin/ Shutterstock Inc., (bottom) CP Photo - Ryan White; p. 28: Denis Selivanov/Shutterstock Inc.; p. 29: CP Photo; p. 31: Barrett & MacKay/AllCanadaPhotos.com; p. 32: RVN/Alamy; p. 33: (both) Henry Georgi/ AllCanadaPhotos.com; p. 34: Rob Howard/Corbis; p. 35: Duncan de Young/Shutterstock Inc.; p. 36: Bettmann/Corbis; p. 37: (left) Keller & Keller Photography/Stock Food Canada, (right) Brett Mulcahy/Shutterstock Inc.; p. 38: Henry Georgi/Shutterstock Inc.; p. 39: Shenval/Alamy; p. 40: Library and Archives Canada/PA-061741; p. 41: (top) Jan Butchofsky-Houser/Corbis, (bottom) Barrett & MacKay/ AllCanadaPhotos.com; p. 42: (top) Canada Dept. of Interior/Library and Archives Canada/C-000284, (top right) The Canadian Press/Tom Hanson, (bottom) The Canadian Press/Andrew Vaughan; p. 43: (top) Blickwinkel/Alamy, (bottom) Mary Evans Picture Library/Alamy.

Produced by Plan B Book Packagers
Editorial: Ellen Rodger
Design: Rosie Gowsell-Pattison
Special thanks to consultant and editor Terrance Cox, adjunct professor, Brock University; Adrianna Morganelli; Tanya Rutledge; Jim Chernishenko.

Library and Archives Canada Cataloguing in Publication

Gleason, Carrie, 1973-
Nova Scotia / Carrie Gleason.
(Canada close up)
ISBN 978-0-545-98908-4
1. Nova Scotia--Juvenile literature.
I. Title. II. Series: Canada close up (Toronto, Ont.)
FC2311.2.G54 2009   j971.6   C2009-900235-3

ISBN-10 0-545-98908-6

6 5 4 3 2 1   Printed in Canada   09 10 11 12 13 14

Welcome to Nova Scotia!

Welcome to "down east"! Nova Scotia is the heart of Canada's **maritime** region. Almost an island, it is attached to New Brunswick by an **isthmus**. It is Canada's second-smallest province, but what it lacks in size, it makes up for in its rich, seafaring past and toe-tapping, fiddle-playing culture.

In Nova Scotia you may be invited to a kitchen party, to a cottage on a rocky shore or for a drive along a scenic coast. Look out to sea and you might spot the billowing sails of the *Bluenose II,* a replica of a grand wooden schooner – a sailing ship of the early 1900s. The *Bluenose II* is Nova Scotia's **ambassador**. She sails North America's east coast and the St. Lawrence River to remind all who see her to visit friendly Nova Scotia.

Chapter 1
Surrounded by Sea

No place in Nova Scotia is more than an hour's drive from the sea. Its mainland is a **peninsula** along Canada's Atlantic coast. The deep, narrow Strait of Canso separates the mainland from its largest island, Cape Breton. Over 50 years ago a **causeway** was built to connect the island to the mainland. Now people can drive to it instead of taking a boat.

An automated lighthouse overlooks the Atlantic Ocean. Nova Scotia has more lighthouses than any other province. The oldest working lighthouse in North America was built here in 1758.

Fishing boats sit at low tide on the Bay of Fundy mud.

The Bay of Fundy

Except at the 24-kilometre-wide Isthmus of Chignecto, the Bay of Fundy divides Nova Scotia from New Brunswick. In the bay cruise minke, humpback, fin and northern right whales.

The Bay of Fundy splits into two inlets, Chignecto Bay and the Minas Basin, like a two-pronged fork. Twice a day, tides raise the water level in the Bay of Fundy – especially in the Minas Basin. Here, the water rises as much as sixteen metres – the world's highest recorded tides! When the tides go out, mud flats reveal molluscs such as clams, mussels and scallops on the basin floor. These wetland habitats attract birds like sandpipers, bald eagles and peregrine falcons.

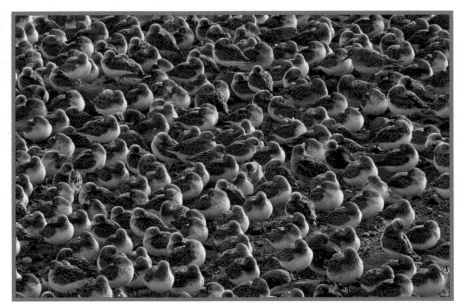

Migrating semipalmated sandpipers wait for low tide to gorge on mud shrimp in the Minas Basin.

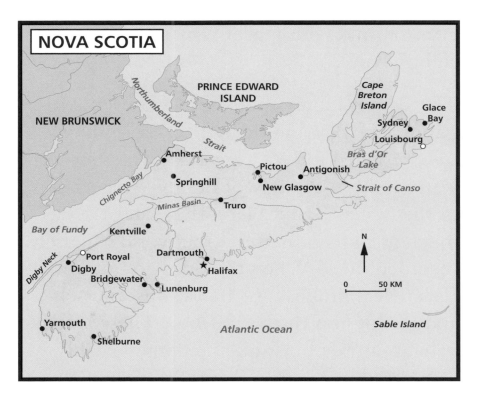

NOVA SCOTIA

PRINCE EDWARD ISLAND

Cape Breton Island

Glace Bay

Sydney

NEW BRUNSWICK

Northumberland Strait

Louisbourg

Bras d'Or Lake

Amherst

Pictou

Antigonish

Springhill

New Glasgow

Strait of Canso

Chignecto Bay

Minas Basin

Truro

Bay of Fundy

Kentville

N

Digby Neck

Port Royal

Dartmouth

Digby

Halifax

Bridgewater

Lunenburg

0   50 KM

Yarmouth

Atlantic Ocean

Sable Island

Shelburne

The coasts

The Northumberland Strait lies off the north shore of the province. Here rolling hills meet sandy beaches. On Nova Scotia's western coastline, the steep cliffs of the Minas Basin rise out of the water to form the shore. To the south, the Digby Neck, a five-kilometre–wide peninsula that runs along the mainland, breaks up the coastline. The Digby Neck has many small fishing communities known for their scallop fishing fleets.

The eastern coastline faces the Atlantic Ocean. Winds blowing in off the ocean and waves pounding the shore have shaped it into bays and hidden coves.

The Digby wharf is home to scallopers, draggers, trawlers, seiners and Cape Islanders – all fishing vessels.

Rocky uplands

Nova Scotia has high, rocky areas called uplands and lower-lying areas called lowlands. The southern upland is the largest. Here, in south and central Nova Scotia, there are many rivers, lakes and thick forests that are home to beavers, deer, porcupines and bears.

The North Mountain, which runs along the Bay of Fundy, is an upland area that was created by volcanic activity millions of years ago. The Cobequid Hills lie just north of the Minas Basin. This upland area is part of the Appalachian mountain range that extends along the east coast of North America. The Pictou-Antigonish Highlands in the east are heavily forested and home to moose and other animals. Rising taller than all the others are the Cape Breton Highlands.

The rocky cliffs of Cap d'Or on the Bay of Fundy

Fertile lowlands

The many small lowland areas have good, fertile soil for farming. The Annapolis Valley lies between the North Mountain and the southern uplands along the Bay of Fundy. This lowland area is the most important farming region in the province. The Northumberland lowlands, in the north, are mostly marshy. Other lowland areas include the area around the Minas Basin and southern Cape Breton Island.

The most common wetlands in Nova Scotia are bogs. Bogs are soggy, flat areas covered in mosses. Blueberries and cranberries can grow in bogs.

Sable Island

Sable Island lies off the east coast of Nova Scotia. The island is an enormous crescent-shaped sandbar surrounded by **shoals**. It was once known as the "Graveyard of the Atlantic" because, before the use of **radar**, more than 350 ships sank or ran aground here during storms. About 250 years ago, horses were brought to the island. Today, their wild descendants are the only permanent residents.

The warm Gulf Stream meets the cold Labrador Current and creates a fog that rolls in from the sea.

Fogs and nor'easters

The weather changes often in Nova Scotia and what comes next can be a surprise. The summers are mostly sunny and warm, but cooler near the coasts. This is because the cold waters of the Atlantic help cool the air. When this air is damp, thick fog blankets the coasts. The fog is especially common in spring and early summer.

On the northern mainland and Cape Breton Island, winters are long and cold. Every place in the province can be affected by fierce winter storms called nor'easters.

Nova Scotia numbers

- Nova Scotia is the second–smallest province in Canada, with a total area of 55,284 square kilometres.

- In addition to Cape Breton Island, the province includes over 3800 smaller islands.

- The highest point is in the Cape Breton Highlands at White Hill Lake, 532 metres above sea level.

- Nova Scotia's population is 934,405 – the largest of the Maritime provinces. Most people live in cities and towns along the coast.

Halifax port as viewed from Dartmouth

Chapter 2
Nova Scotia's Past

Archeologists believe Nova Scotia's first inhabitants arrived about 11,000 years ago. These people, now called Paleo-Indians, were following migrating caribou. By 5500 BC, the Maritime Archaic Indians lived in what is now Nova Scotia. They fished and hunted seals and other large sea mammals.

The Mi'kmaq

The descendants of the Maritime Archaic Indians are the Mi'kmaq. They moved from place to place with the seasons. In spring they settled near the coasts to take advantage of the plentiful supply of fish and shellfish close by. When cold weather came, they split into family groups and moved farther inland to winter hunting grounds. Today, the Mi'kmaq make up less than one per cent of the population of Nova Scotia. Most live on one of the province's thirteen **reserves**. They have worked to keep their culture, language and history alive.

The Mi'kmaq used birchbark canoes to travel around and across the Bay of Fundy.

European explorers

John Cabot

About 1000 years ago, the **Norse** from Greenland may have become the first Europeans to visit Nova Scotia. In 1497 explorer John Cabot sailed along the North American coast while looking for a route to China, and claimed the land for England. Thirty-seven years later, in 1534, Jacques Cartier explored the area and claimed it for France. England and France had both claimed the same land!

Lured by fish

Cabot's return to Europe with reports of seas filled with fish spurred fishing vessels from Spain, Portugal, England and France to cross the Atlantic. The fishermen traded blankets, cloth, copper kettles and iron tools for the Mi'kmaq's furs. Few men came ashore, and the ships sailed back to Europe in the fall.

In 1604 French fishermen set up a fishing station at Canso, on the western tip of the mainland. Here, fish were brought ashore to be dried before being shipped back to France. This drying method changed little over the next 300 years.

French settlement

Samuel de Champlain

Port Royal was Nova Scotia's first French settlement, and one of the first permanent European settlements in North America. Founded in 1605 by Pierre Du Gua de Monts and Samuel de Champlain, it was a step up from the **scurvy** and misery of an earlier winter spent on Saint Croix Island across the Bay of Fundy.

Here, they built a walled *habitation* where up to 100 men lived for almost three years. They spent their time fishing, growing crops, trapping animals for furs and forming a friendship with the Mi'kmaq.

During the winter of 1606–1607, Champlain established the Order of Good Cheer, assigning responsibility for feasts and entertainment to the men to lift their spirits. When the king of France took away de Monts' rights to the land in 1607, the settlement was abandoned. Later, it was burned by the English.

Port Royal was burned by the English in 1613.

France lost Acadia in 1713, but maintained territory on Cape Breton Island, then known as Île Royale. Construction on the Fortress of Louisbourg began in 1718. The fortress was lost to the English in 1758. It was reconstructed as a National Historic Site in 1961.

L'Acadie

Some French settlers eventually returned to the area around the Bay of Fundy. They built homes, and earth dikes to control the water so they could farm. More people from France joined them. The colony was called *l'Acadie*.

The settlers traded goods with the New England colonists to the south. They also relied on the Mi'kmaq for help. By 1687 the settlement had swelled to 2000 people.

Vying for power

While the French-speaking Acadian population grew, English-speaking people also began to settle here. Scottish settlers arrived in 1622. They called their colony Nova Scotia, which is Latin for New Scotland. England and France had a long history of wars in Europe and a **rivalry** for the New World broke out. Nova Scotia passed between English and French control nine times from 1604 to 1710. By 1713 all of Acadia except for Cape Breton and P.E.I. was under English rule.

The Great Upheaval

As the years passed, the Acadians became less concerned with who ruled them. The English, eager to extend their control over Nova Scotia, encouraged their own settlements to grow. They feared that the Acadians would side with France if war broke out again. By 1753 there were more Acadians in Nova Scotia than British settlers. In 1755 the British governor of the colony, Charles Lawrence, demanded that the Acadians sign an oath of loyalty to England. When the Acadians refused, he ordered that they be removed from Nova Scotia.

Red-coated English army officers read the Decree of Expulsion to Acadian men and boys gathered in a church in 1755.

Le Grand Dérangement was a time of great sorrow as families and friends were separated and deported.

It was a shocking decision. Soldiers raided Acadian settlements, burning homes and fields. More than 10,000 Acadians were packed onto ships destined for British colonies farther south, the Caribbean or France. One-third of those deported died of disease. Acadians call this *le Grand Dérangement,* or the Great Upheaval.

Halifax was settled by the British in 1749 as a military base. The star-shaped citadel that sits on a hill overlooking the city's harbour was built in 1856.

The Grand-Pré historic site is a park that commemorates Acadian heritage in Nova Scotia. A statue of Evangeline, the fictional heroine in a poem written by American poet Henry Wadsworth Longfellow in 1847, was erected on lands Acadians were forced to leave.

Peopling the colony

Immigration from New England was encouraged after the Acadian expulsion. Eight thousand New England **planters** arrived in Nova Scotia from 1760 to 1774. Beginning in 1760 many immigrants also came from England, Scotland, Ireland, Germany and Switzerland.

From 1775 to 1783, while the American colonies were fighting for their independence from Britain, 35,000 people wishing to remain loyal to Britain, called United Empire Loyalists, moved to Nova Scotia. Among them were about 3500 Black Loyalists. They founded Canada's first black settlements.

By 1801 some Acadians also began returning to Nova Scotia. But their numbers were much smaller than before, and they were greatly outnumbered by the new settlers. Today, about eleven per cent of Nova Scotia's population has Acadian ancestry. They live mainly in southern Cape Breton, or along the "French Shore," between Digby and Yarmouth.

Toward Confederation

From 1826 to 1840, Nova Scotia's population doubled. Halifax grew into a busy port city. In 1839 the first railway was built by a mining company near Pictou for hauling coal. Other industries also wanted a railway to ship their goods faster and farther. But it was too expensive for Nova Scotia to build on its own. In 1867 Nova Scotia united with New Brunswick, Canada East (Quebec) and Canada West (Ontario) to become the Dominion of Canada. This event is called Confederation.

Millions of immigrants to Canada first landed at Pier 21 in Halifax before making their way to other parts of the country.

The Halifax Explosion

Halifax was a booming military city when it was flattened on December 6, 1917, by the biggest man–made disaster in Canadian history. Two ships, the *Imo* and the *Mont-Blanc*, collided in Halifax Harbour. The impact started a fire on board the *Mont-Blanc*, which was carrying explosives. When the ship blew up, the blast destroyed most of the city. Two thousand people lost their lives, and another 9000 were injured.

The northern part of Halifax was completely destroyed by the explosion. Many survivors were forced to move, with what little they had left, into tents. Their homes had either been flattened or declared unsafe.

The luxury liner *Olympic* was painted in a form of camouflage called razzle dazzle and converted into a troopship during World War I. Troopships carried soldiers overseas and docked regularly at Halifax Harbour.

Two world wars

During **World War I** and **World War II**, Halifax became a base for shipping troops, weapons, food and war supplies to Europe. But the period between the wars was a time of **economic depression**. Steel plants closed, miners faced pay cuts and times were tough. To create jobs, the government started paving the roads and promoting tourism.

Changing times

After World War II there were more changes for Nova Scotia. In 1959 the St. Lawrence Seaway opened, rerouting much of the transatlantic shipping traffic from Halifax to Montreal. At the same time, coal mining began to decline and steel plants in Cape Breton closed. The poor economy meant that many Nova Scotians left the province to find work elsewhere. In the 1990s fish stocks declined, putting many fishers and processing plant employees out of work.

Today, tourism has helped Nova Scotia's economy recover. So has better management of natural resources such as fish and trees.

The fishing port of Lunenburg attracts many tourists.

Chapter 3

From Land and Sea

Nova Scotia's natural resources, such as trees, minerals, animals and soil, have played an important role in its economy, its culture and its past.

The ocean's riches

Being surrounded by water means that Nova Scotians take advantage of the sea's bounty. The Scotian Shelf is an area of raised sea floor off the east coast where nutrient-rich waters attract marine life. It is an important fishing ground. Others are the Gulf of St. Lawrence and the Bay of Fundy.

The main catch is groundfish, such as haddock, cod, pollock and halibut, that live near the sea floor. Herring, mackerel, bluefin tuna and capelin are also fished in great numbers. But the sea creature that brings in the most money is lobster. Nova Scotia is the world's biggest lobster exporter.

Today haddock and lobster are the big catches.

About seventeen per cent of the money Nova Scotia makes from exports to other countries comes from the sale of fish. The fishing industry provides jobs on fishing boats and in processing plants, where fish is canned or made into products like fish burgers and fish sticks.

Mineral mining

Some of Nova Scotia's most important natural resources are from underground. A vast salt deposit lies beneath Pugwash, a village in the north. Gypsum, a chalky mineral that comes from evaporated salt water, is extracted from quarries in the north and on Cape Breton Island. Nova Scotia is the world's biggest producer of gypsum. Limestone, quartz, silica, marble, gravel and peat are also mined around the province.

King coal

Coal is a hard, black substance that is burned as fuel in power plants. It is an important Nova Scotia resource. Coalfields lie underground in the north, and on Cape Breton Island. Many small communities grew up around coal mines because of the jobs they provided. But coal mining is dirty and dangerous. In 2001 the last underground coal mine in Nova Scotia closed. There are three coal mines in Nova Scotia today, and they are all above ground.

Disaster strikes

In the 1830s coal was discovered in Springhill, Nova Scotia. But the human cost of the **prosperity** that the coal mines brought to the community was high. Many men and boys lost their lives in "the pit." In 1891 a fire in the mine killed 125 people. Thirty–nine miners were killed in an explosion in 1956 in the same mine. Two years later, another 74 miners died in a cave–in. The Springhill mine closed in 1959, but these mining disasters remain as some of Canada's worst.

Rescue miners called draegermen haul out a miner on a stretcher during the 1958 Springhill disaster. Some miners were trapped underground for ten days.

Tidal energy

Nova Scotians have developed a way to create clean energy using a resource that won't run out – the extreme tides of the Bay of Fundy. The Annapolis Tidal Generating Station was built in the 1980s on a causeway over the Annapolis River. Engineers dammed the river to trap the tidewaters. The force of the water powers a turbine that creates electricity for about 4000 homes. It is one of only three tidal power stations in the world.

The shipyards

The logging industry in Nova Scotia created another industry – shipbuilding. Large hardwood trees cut down in the 1800s were used to build ships that would then transport timber and fish to Europe. Yarmouth and Pictou were both important shipbuilding centres. In time, Nova Scotia built up one of the largest shipping fleets in the world. When iron steamships began to take over, many of Nova Scotia's shipyards closed. Today, some builders still operate shipyards along the coasts.

Only about eight per cent of Nova Scotia's land is used for farming. The province is known for its apples, pears, potatoes, squash and pumpkins, which are harvested in the fall.

Farming

Most farms along the Northumberland Strait and the Minas Basin are dairy and poultry farms. The Annapolis Valley has nutrient-rich soil good for growing fruit, especially apples.

Manufacturing

Many Nova Scotians today work in manufacturing, making goods that are exported to other places. These jobs are in food processing plants, pulp and paper mills, sawmills and building supply companies. Some large companies have set up factories that make tires and auto parts.

Chapter 4
Community Ties

Nova Scotia's early settlers built their communities around family groups or nationality. Most Nova Scotians today have Scottish, English or Irish roots. As immigration from Asia, Africa and Eastern Europe has grown, the province has become more **diverse** and multicultural.

Haligonians

About 40 per cent of the people in Nova Scotia live in the capital and largest urban area, Halifax. They are known as Haligonians. The city's waterfront has many restaurants and museums. Some streets are lined with historic wooden houses painted in bright colours.

A Scottish piper in green tartan performs at the Dartmouth Multicultural Festival.

Downtown Halifax is a lively area of office buildings, shops and pubs where folk music is often played.

Service with a smile

About 75 per cent of jobs in Nova Scotia are in the service industry – in banks, schools, hospitals and government. Tourism is also big business. Over one million visitors are drawn to Nova Scotia each year, spending their money at local hotels, stores and restaurants.

The Old Town Clock in Halifax was built in 1803.

Africville

North Halifax was once home to a community of people descended from Black Loyalists from the United States. The community became known as Africville. Living conditions were poor, and those who found work were paid low wages because they were black. In the 1960s, the residents were relocated and the area was levelled by bulldozers to make way for the expanding city of Halifax.

Stories in art

In folk music there are clues to the way life was lived in the past. Nova Scotia's folk songs tell the stories of the people who settled here. Stan Rogers was a well-known and well-loved folk musician and songwriter with roots in Nova Scotia. The Stan Rogers Folk Festival in Canso now attracts performers from all over the world.

Worn wool clothing was cut into strips to make colourful and durable hooked rugs. Now wool yarn is used as well.

Just as folk music tells stories of the past, the work produced by Nova Scotia's many artists shows a glimpse of life here too. Folk art was first created by farmers and fishermen in their free time. Rustic woodcarvings of people, animals, fish or boats are painted in bright colours. Often the figures have a humorous twist.

Since the 1930s, hooked rugs handmade in the Acadian community of Chéticamp have been prized for their beautiful workmanship, colour and design.

Down by the sea

The sea is inescapable in Nova Scotia life and culture. Many ballads have been sung of ships lost at sea. Some grand old seaside homes have a widow's walk, a small balcony where a sea captain's wife might watch anxiously for her husband's return.

In the early 1900s, fishermen boarded schooners to sail to the cod fishing grounds in the north Atlantic. They fished from small boats called dories, which were towed or stowed by the schooners.

Today small, quaint fishing villages still line the Nova Scotia coast. Many of them now house restaurants and shops for tourists.

Fishermen haul cod onto the deck of a wooden schooner, wearing waterproof clothing including sou'westers, rain hats with wide brims.

Seafood and more

At one time, seafood was the dinner of fishermen and the poor. But today seafood is popular with everyone. Plunged into a pot or filling a sandwich called a "roll," lobster is a common menu item. Other locally caught seafood includes scallops, mussels and clams, all of which can be added to a piping hot, creamy seafood chowder. Digby is famous for its scallops, a type of mollusc. It is also known for "Digby chicks," fillets of smoked herring. For landlubbers, rappie pie or *pâté à la râpure* is a traditional Acadian dish made with chicken or beef and grated potatoes, and baked in the oven like a pie.

A lobster roll makes a tasty lunch.

Chowder, a hearty soup, can be created from leftover bits of seafood.

The Cabot Trail is a scenic road that winds through Cape Breton Highlands National Park.

Chapter 5
Cape Breton Island

Cape Breton Island is Nova Scotia's crowning jewel. Spectacular highlands cover the northern part of the island. Along the outer edge runs the Cabot Trail, swooping along dramatic coastal cliffs. Cape Breton Highlands National Park is a protected area of green wilderness where people can hike and camp.

Highlanders

Ciad Mile Failte (KEE-ad MEEL-aa FALL-cha) is a Cape Breton greeting. It means "one hundred thousand welcomes" in the Gaelic language — the language of the Scottish Highlands.

Most of Cape Breton's early settlers were highland farmers from Scotland who were thrown off their land to make way for sheep farms. Their Scottish heritage has been kept alive on Cape Breton Island by its **isolation** and its rugged highlands.

At St. Ann's Bay, the Gaelic College of Celtic Arts and Crafts teaches people about the language, traditional crafts, music and dance of the Scottish Highlanders.

Highland dancers, in traditional tartan costume and shoes called *ghillies*, often compete at festivals of Scottish culture called Highland Games.

Musical gatherings

Kitchen parties are a Nova Scotia tradition, especially in rural Cape Breton. Here, people gather in the kitchen to play music, enjoy a drink and tell stories.

A *ceilidh* (KAY-lee) is a Gaelic concert held at a local hall or a pub. People in a community come together to be entertained by musicians and storytellers. Traditionally, people gathered for *ceilidhs* in a neighbour's home after their evening chores were done.

A famous summer resident

For 40 years Alexander Graham Bell, inventor of the telephone, spent his summers at Baddeck on Cape Breton Island. The first flight of the *Silver Dart*, built with his help, was from the frozen surface of Baddeck Bay in 1909.

The *Silver Dart* was the first powered aircraft to fly in Canada.

The shimmering Bras d'Or Lake is a huge saltwater lake that nearly cuts Cape Breton in half.

Sydney is Cape Breton's largest city and one of the province's industrial centres. Coal mining and steelmaking have played an important role in its history.

Chapter 6
Points of Pride

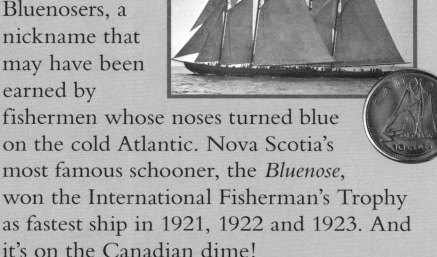

▶ Nova Scotians are known as Bluenosers, a nickname that may have been earned by fishermen whose noses turned blue on the cold Atlantic. Nova Scotia's most famous schooner, the *Bluenose*, won the International Fisherman's Trophy as fastest ship in 1921, 1922 and 1923. And it's on the Canadian dime!

▶ Nova Scotia has a thriving and lively music culture. World-famous singers Anne Murray, Sarah McLachlan and Holly Cole come from Nova Scotia, as did country music legend Hank Snow. Fiddlers Ashley MacIsaac and Natalie MacMaster began their careers playing at Cape Breton dances.

▶ The lighthouse at Peggy's Cove, a picturesque fishing village, is a world-famous Nova Scotia icon. Every summer it serves as a post office — the only one in a lighthouse in all of North America.

▶ The French fortress of Louisbourg on Cape Breton Island dates to the early 1700s when the area belonged to France. In the 1960s it was reconstructed and made a National Historic Site.

▶ Samuel Cunard of Halifax started a steamship business in 1838 that became one of the world's biggest and most famous transatlantic shipping companies.

Glossary

ambassador: Usually a person, but sometimes an object, used to promote or represent a place

causeway: A raised road across a body of water

diverse: Varied

economic depression: A time of hardship brought on by a financial and industrial slump

habitation: A structure in which to live

isolation: Separation from other parts of the country

isthmus: A narrow strip of land that connects two large areas of land

maritime: Connected with the sea

Norse: Ancient Scandinavians or Vikings

peninsula: An area of land that is surrounded by water on three sides

planters: Colonists or settlers

prosperity: Wealth and success

radar: A system that reflects high-frequency radio waves to detect the position and speed of ships, aircraft, etc.

reserves: Designated land set aside for First Nations peoples to live on

rivalry: Competition for the same objective

scurvy: A disease caused by lack of vitamin C, that leads to bleeding gums, loose teeth, sores and even death

shoals: Areas of shallow water with submerged sandbanks

World War I: An international conflict (1914-1918) that took place largely in Europe, and in which an estimated ten million lives were lost

World War II: An international conflict (1939-1945) that spread throughout Europe, North Africa, southeast Asia and the western Pacific, and claimed the lives of an estimated 55 million people